CHEAP THE CHANGE

By

SEAN CHRISTOPHER

CHEAP THE CHANGE

Designed by Sean Christopher

While inspired by real events and historical characters, this is a work of non-fiction and it does not claim to be historically accurate or portray factual events or relationships. Bear in mind, actual persons, living or dead, business

ISBN: 978-1-948688-13-0

Printed in the U.S.A

First Publication, 2018

DISCLAIMER

This book is written for information purposes only. Every effort was made to make this book as complete and accurate as possible. This book provides information only up to the publishing date. Therefore, this book should be used as a guide - not as the ultimate source.

The purpose of this book is to educate. The author and the publisher does not warrant that the information contained in this book is fully complete and shall not be responsible for any errors or omissions.

The author and publisher shall have neither liability nor responsibility to any person or entity with respect to any loss or damage caused or alleged to be caused directly or indirectly by this book.

ABOUT THE AUTHOR

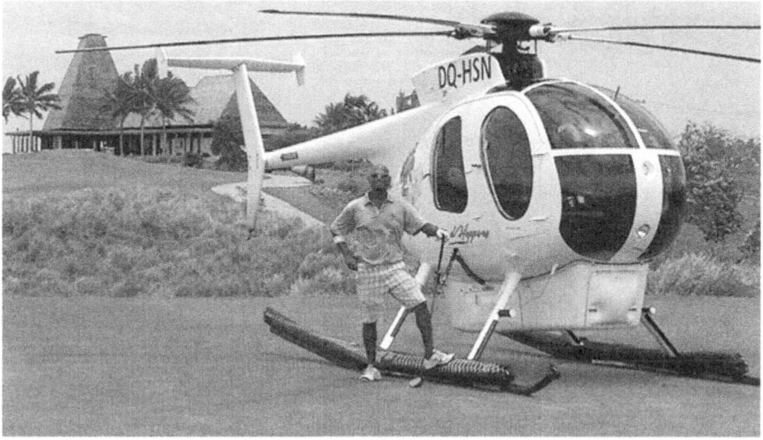

Sean Christopher is an American author. He resides in Las Vegas, Nevada, and has traveled to over 35 countries. He is an avid sports enthusiast, intellectual, and innovator. He is a serial entrepreneur, and is the founder of the website www.cheapthechange.com, the entertainer known as Coolie Mac, and the writer of the song: “Famous.”

QUOTE

"The literacy of earning is learning."

– Sean Christopher

TABLE OF CONTENTS

PROLOGUE

Cheap the Change is a straightforward methodology that will provide you power for living. You will only need one hour to read this book. Why read a novel when you can get all that you need in one quick read, and be empowered at the same time? The 21st century is about empowerment. You cannot use what you do not have. Education must be passed down. If you are reading this book than I personally thank you, and I hope it blesses you, so you may logically grow sensible as a person. I have abridged my thoughts into fifteen categories that will provide you endless wisdom, so that you can be the best person you can be. Life is about winning, so win big and do well. That is my anticipation for you.

POEM

Who's next in line?
All these fools come and go!
They play but pay while they lose their way.
The game is to be sold, while, not to be told.
That is how the wise are to be defined.
The sensible ponder, but never do they squander.
The practical lend instead of recklessly spend.
The thrifty turn wealthy because they live very healthy.
And all the rest couldn't care less
Because what can you do,
When it's all gone and you lose?
It's your choice,
So what will you choose?

CHAPTER 1: *CHEAP IT; DON'T KEEP IT*

"Whoever brings blessing will be enriched, and one who waters will himself be watered."[i]

The word "cheap" gets a bad rap in society. It's considered a bad word like a mucky expletive. For some reason cheap has been associated with "low value," "it sucks," or "it's not good enough." Ironically, in our society we are led to believe that cheap is a word that rich people avoid when all actuality affluent people know the true meaning of the word: cheap. Cheap in its truest definition means, "Low in price or worth more than its cost."[ii] That's not a bad thing at all. Why in fact, that sounds like a bargain!

Actually, the cold hard truth is that "cheap" has been obliterated in the English language because it's an attack on savvy shoppers who know how to bargain hunt. The reason this five-letter word "cheap" has been attacked so passionately is because it's the key to success. Interestingly, the term has also been used to verbally attack a person like, "He's so cheap! Or I don't date cheap men. That's cheap!"

What's ironic about the "user" who dislikes a cheap person is the reality that the so-called "user" can't leech off of the judicious person for their money. Cheapness is a line of defense, like a well-mended fence that keeps intruders at bay, while not making an offense. There is a saying, *"if you give all the beggars your money you will become a beggar too."* There needs to be prudence in your dealings. It's like seeing Las Vegas beggars asking for your money on the Strip. Is that really a tangible way to earn a living? It would be an interesting study to research why Person X associates with Person Y in the first place. It's so they can benefit from them. That's the whole point of having a social circle in the first place. Networking, anyone?

Could it be possible that the very persons who are attacking the so-called cheap person are cheap themselves because they have never hosted anything in their lives? How ironic it is when cheaper poor people attack cheap rich people who worked hard to be rich? Now, who's really being cheap? You see where this is going? *Cheapness* is a mean word when used in or out of context. Being cheap can be a bad thing when you are not generous when you can be. However, being cheap is actually the key to generosity, because the buck has to stop somewhere so the saved surplus can be used for better advancements. Cheaply made is the problem if it can't stand the test of time, but cheaply bought is a whole other story. Buying cheap is how you win.

Cheap it; don't keep it simply means to acquire inexpensively so you may have more to be generous with. Especially, when it matters in the long run. Advertisements are created to do the opposite. If they have a hold on your pocket book, how will you have a surplus for the people you truly love?

Redistribution of wealth only works when you don't keep it but you cheap it, so you have more money to give. How does a philanthropist give money if he does not have any? At some point, he must give up something to get something in return.

CHAPTER 2: *QUICK MONEY PARTS*

"The wealth of the sinner is stored up for the righteous."[iii]

Have you heard the term, "A fool and his money part quickly?" This statement is the direct attack on profligates, the spendthrifts who fail in practicing the art of frugality. Frugality is an art form. It's a discipline. It means self–restraint. Prudence is the practice of self-denial. In its strongest definition the word means pure abstinence. It's in this self-restraint where the pennywise negotiator stamps his ticket to fortune. That is the essence of cheap living. Living cheaply is much different than cheapening life because you don't want to pay the pied piper.

Robbing Peter to pay Paul is what the squanderer does. The reciprocal to money that parts quickly is, “A wise man and his money live together.” It basically means the relationship of fidelity between the two is chummy when compared to other suitors who are trying to create an adulterous relationship. That is the “others” who try to invade your mind to separate you and your pie.

Instead of robbing Peter or Paul you might as well sell to John or James, and keep selling to Matthew and Nathaniel. This way the consumers want to gladly give you their money because you are providing a grand ole service. Poor service means poor earnings. Rich service leads to high earnings.

CHAPTER 3: *SELL SOMETHING*

"Buy truth, and do not sell it, Get wisdom and instruction and understanding."[iv]

If you can't sell, your pocket won't swell. How's that for a rhyme? Make a nickel into a dime and save your time for some sunshine. Isn't it great when money is in the bank? And, all of your bills are paid. Thanks! The good Lord is great, and keep making your cake before the daybreak because there will be days when your investments won't pan out either. Sometimes it's better to have love and not sell it neither. The art of the start is to not part with your heart, but keep playing the game and even if you strike out, keep swinging for fame because when you connect it's going to be a shot, like a home run ball out of the park!

Why sell for others when you can sell yourself? Sell to earn and sell to learn.

Commoditizing your being is the way to do this. The power to sell yourself is the power to get them paying. Strippers do this! Hahaha, but you don't want to strip. There are other avenues to get the same thing.

Write a book. Make a song. Paint a portrait. Shoot a film. Sell your stuff. Make it and sell it. Get good at this because you will be doing it for the rest of your life, if you plan on being an entrepreneur. There's no way to the green way without the real way, which is the retail highway. If you are good than sell your goods. 3 words to learn: "At your service." So what are you serving? You can't sell what you don't have. It's either a good or a service so figure it out.

Chapter 4: *Rich Friends and Tens*

"Come, let us deal wisely with them, or else."[v]

Tens make friends with rich people. If you are a dime, than you are an asset and people will want your time. Rent yourself for a price, and you will be in the money. Because time is money, spend your time wisely with those who will give you perks, perquisites, and privileges. Tens do this. They know how to hob nob with the rich. It's like charging your cell phone to your laptop. You need some of their energy, so take it freely by getting plugged in. Once you are charged up, you get to charge others up.

If you have to spend money on a woman to have her love you, well, you don't have a real relationship. Men who have a "real" woman don't spend money for sex. You need to understand what I mean. Paying for sex is transactional sex, but it's not love sex. You get love sex when a woman falls in love with you. Certain men make women fall in love with them without money. That's when your game is on point.

Women fall in love with you when you get in their mind. That's it. That's all you have to do. It's the brain tease. It's nothing more than that. If you can get into her mind you have her won. Meeting her emotional need for love and validation is what a ten does. Money is not required. Money is simply a lure. Fish on!

CHAPTER 5: *LOSS VEGAS*

"After he had spent everything, there was a severe famine in that whole country, and he began to be in need."[vi]

Have you been to Las Vegas? Well, it should be called "Loss" Vegas because that's all that happens here. All the "lostitutes" are just losing their money[vii]. "Lostitution" is a common practice here in Sin City.[viii] Vegas were built on losers not on winners. 80% of the people in this town are losers (good people, just not winners at the casino). How else would the Casinos make a dime? The casino operators realized quickly they could make a fortune on gamblers.[ix] Don't gamble. You are not going to win. It's not a good idea. Don't be a loser. Poker is different because it's a skills game versus fallible human beings. Gambling is losing when the odds are completely against you.

You want contrarian advice than here it is. Play and lose. See how fun that is? There is nothing wrong with having fun. Just remember it's expensive entertainment. Losing is not fun. When has it ever been? I'm still annoyed about my little league baseball team losing in the Florida state finals back in 1994.[x] I hate losing. In fact, the best advice I ever got in Las Vegas was by a blackjack dealer at the Palm's Casino who told me, "Kid, give it up. This is not the road to wealth." His word still echoes in my soul. So I don't play anymore. I walked.

The key to winning is "never play their game" because if you do you will lose. Their system is rigged. The architects of the games are designed to make you lose. The key to "winning" is to *play your game*. If you cannot avoid the vices you will remain a loser.

You must be shrewd in this world if you want to win big in the money game. It happens when you don't gamble but you create assets. Once again, no one is saying "don't play" but if you are going to play why don't you play when you have a ton of money and losing on tiny hands is trivial. That way there is no stress to make money at the tables. Trying to make money at the tables is not a good idea. Suggestion: *don't gamble*.

CHAPTER 6: *PRAY IT; DON'T SPRAY IT*

"And all things you ask in prayer, believing, you will receive."[xi]

I kid you not. I can't make this up. It's not in my blood; I wouldn't do that. It's also against my religion. See that nice hat I am wearing in the photo. What if I told you, I bought that nice fedora for only 2 bucks. Yep. I barely paid anything for it. It was not a present either. I got it on the cheap. How did I do that?

Well, first of all, I was praying real intently to God for a deal! Truth be told, I don't like buying things on a whim. I am a purposed shopper. However, there are times when what you want is nowhere to be found. So you have to keep digging.

I'm stubborn. What's wrong about obtaining a fedora for a reasonable price? So many stores are a rip-off! Me, I prefer wholesale or repossession. My first approach was to scour the different Goodwill's in town, however, nothing fit and some of the hats smelled![xii] Gross. Who wants that? Not cool!

Then by happenstance, I was driving to San Diego and about 3 hours into the journey, I stopped at the 99-cent store in San Bernardino for some provisions. As I walked through the shopping lanes, by chance I happened to look into one of the aisles, and to my surprise I could not believe what I saw? A fedora! How in the world was a fedora for sale at the 99-cent store? *No way, dude!* Prayer works.

So I tried on the hat. What do you know? It fit perfectly! I was like "God works!" This idyllic hat fits seamlessly to my noggin. And, it's only 2 bucks! *Cha-ching!* Great deal! Score! What an awesome God! Amen! Hallelujah! I believe! Will the hat last forever? No! But it's good to get things on the cheap that run their course because then I get to buy something else.

Back to the fedora, it was such a big score. I mean it's one thing to have a friend give you a gift, but it's a whole other thing when you coincidentally are walking through a dollar store in California, and you see a fedora that fits perfectly to your head. Isn't Cali supposed to be expensive? *Not this time!* Buying on the cheap is fun, so I bought two! Lesson to be learned: pray to God and he will answer in due season. It's all about timing, having an open mind, and being inquisitive. [xiii]

Chapter 7: *Commoditize Your Being*

"The soil produces crops by itself; first the blade, then the head, then the mature grain in the head."[xiv]

Commoditizing your being is a realism you will face in this life. Essentially, your body is a work engine and when it is put to work it will garner a financial yield, when contracted for labor. However, there are more ways to make money than just labor. In this section, we will discuss a few of these ways.

Short books are what people like to read. Who wants to read a long drawn out book? Just meet the need of your client. Give them what they want. Technology solves many of our problems. You ever heard the phrase, "you are either the problem or the solution" so be the solution. Our culture is rough. Basically, losers don't make money. Winners make money. The most innovative people are the performers who you see that have talent to showcase.

Here's the solution: if you don't commodify your being you will go broke. Then you will have to be dirt-cheap and nobody will want to hang around you. You see all of those bums in the tunnels of Las Vegas. That's not where you want to be. While at the South Point Casino, I attended the Dennis Bono show with a friend.[xv] It was fun, I saw the hostess dressed in a Brazilian Carnival outfit at the front entrance. I thought to myself, "what's the reason they go to great lengths to have her work here?" I rationalized it's because she was part of the show. She was a performer. She was part of the attraction. I learned a very important lesson that day. Be an attraction. *Get to the center of the act.* You get the hint?

CHAPTER 8: *SLEEP AND MAKE MONEY*

"Ants are creatures of little strength, yet they store up their food in the summer."[xvi]

A small investment in a solid investment vehicle can turn into millions. It's all about planting a seed. The more you plant the larger the harvest. Why be a stressed out day trader? That's pointless. To sleep and make money all you must do is purposely invest and just wait a year later and see your investment grow. There is no need to be concerned.

The hardest lesson to learn is to let your money ride. If you let it ride, the investment has a chance to quintuple or even shoot up twenty times in its original value. The money can't stay in your hand. You must give it wings to fly. You can't hold your money too tightly or it will never leave your hand. You can't bring it back to you too quickly or it won't fully mature and you will lose the huge windfall. The key is to plant early and just wait.[xvii]

This is called, "[Casting] your bread upon the waters."[xviii] With that said, you cannot just throw your money anywhere like on a dartboard. You must plant your money in fertile soil. Fertile soil is an investment where everyone also has the "confidence" to invest. When the singularity of investor confidence arrives then you will sleep and make lots of money.

The key to employ this principle correctly is to invest when something is valued at very little, but has the potential to become the next big thing. Rule of thumb: never invest in anything that is on the high side or you will get burned. Invest when it is on the low side and has great potential to shoot for the sky. It's called the "business cycle."[xix] It must be something that hedge funds and private equity firms want to grab. Your job is to position yourself before them so that you are on the front end of the investment.

CHAPTER 9: *DIFFERENT STAGES OF LIFE*

"While we have opportunity, let us do good to all people."[xx]

You cannot give what you do not have. You must create precedence if you want to have an upward mobile career. This only takes place when you have a *title*, call it a name - the kind of accomplishment or credential to garner recognition worthy of such production. Build that resume baby. Once you have the certification or credentials you may proceed to the next level.

The world is a stage. When you perform well at each new stage of your life you earn the right to play at the next stage, and it will continue like this forever. There's a reason for the seasons. Identifying the season you are in will help you act out the play correctly.

Life is a Shakespearian drama and you get to play all the parts. That is, if you choose too. You are capable of so many things and that happens when you identify the stage while providing a worthy performance. Having the ability to not be the center of attention is central. The best actors know how to perform in each setting regardless of who is looking. In reality, you are always the “central act” because you know how to play different roles without receiving negative attention.

CHAPTER 10: *MAKES CENTS*

"'Well done, good and faithful servant! You have been faithful with a few things; I will put you in charge of many things."[xxi]

Follow the money. If it makes money than it makes cents. Understanding "money creation" is highly important for financial acumen. If you don't study "money creation" it's going to be hard for you to cheap the change. Getting paid works when you understand the different avenues to receive money. Here are some ways to get money:

1) Inheritance
2) Lottery
3) Win A Contest
4) Work Income
5) Residual Income
6) Investment Income
7) Business Income

8) Gift
9) Stealing
10) Marry Up

Stealing is not recommended because it's illegal. The other one's are viable ways to get money. The more income streams you have the better. Your whole life you should be focused on generating income stream after income stream. It's like building a resume. Keep building. Once you have enough streams of income, your reservoir will be full to the brim. A financial shortage is like a water shortage, your streams of income are depleting so to replenish them you must generate more revenue in differing forms. This happens by acquiring or producing product to sell. Imagine, your cash flow stream turning into the Amazon River. This happens with a top quality service or good that your consumer wants. There are only three kinds of business types: builders, middlemen, and investors. Figure out which one you are.

CHAPTER 11: *STANDARD OF LIVING*

"Wise men store up knowledge, But with the mouth of the foolish, ruin is at hand."[xxii]

To live a high standard you must live below your means. There is no other way to explain this. It's imperative you don't get in over yourself or you will go through financial struggle. While kids, cars, homes, vacations, and luxuries are nothing but awesome, they also cost a pretty penny. Running costs will be your death knell. Anything you can buy that involves maintenance or revolving dues will be a negative on your bank ledger.

The way to eliminate running costs is to literally purge yourself of anything that keeps on adding expenses to your life. So if you want a new boat you must know it will require repairs, gasoline, and you will have to renew the tags every year. In addition, your nut will increase if you have a monthly boat slip. Always ask, "Are the running costs worth the investment in the first place?" Time, money, and energy are all you have in this life so use these resources wisely, or you will put yourself in a world of hurt.

Counting the cost will help you evaluate how much risk you want to take on. If it's going to sink your ship than don't do it! Because drowning in debt is not good. You don't want to break even in life. You want to have a superfluous overflow where your vats will brim over with new wine and your barns will be overflowing. This happens when you are content in your soul and you exercise prudence with every financial decision. The two biggest mistakes a person will make is believe when they have money they should spend it, and when they have lots of money not to spend it when it necessitates a high quality of life. There should always be balance in your life. Don't frivolously spend, wisely invest into purpose; you will see a huge difference in the quality of your life.

After your nest egg grows, then begin to make additions to your life: wife, kids, and the *necessaries* that go along with family maintenance. Don't pay for the past, but prepare for the future by presently not getting *caught up*.[xxiii]

CHAPTER 12: *F.U. MONEY*

"King Solomon was richer and wiser than any other king in the world."[xxiv]

There are three kinds of money. There is "breakaway money," that is when you are creating separation from a negative bank balance. The denomination is like $50,000 to $500,000. This type of money sets you up for investments and small business formation.

The next kind of money is "screw you money," which is like 1 to 2 million dollars. If carefully invested properly you could technically retire on this money with rental properties and savvy investments. Money is to be managed properly and it should not be in the hands of fools because all they do is waste it.

The third type of money is "F.U. Money."[xxv] As it is dubbed, this kind of money immediately says, “F.U.” to money, the employer, and everyone else on the planet. Think lottery winners. This is when you have enough money to insulate yourself from bills, debts, obligations, payments, and all other fees of life. Millionaire athletes may quality for F.U. money. Poignantly said, F.U. money is over 10 million in the bank.[xxvi] Once you have this kind of money you are in the top 1 percent of the world. With this kind of money you can do whatever you want in moderation. It does not mean you are god, but it does mean your employer just lost an employee. *Smile*.

Chapter 13: *Wealth Preservation*

"A good man leaves an inheritance to his children's children."[xxvii]

The goal is to get to "F.U. Money," however, that does not give you free license to spend your way to poverty. You'd be surprised how many times the singularity has happened to people who have *some* money. You still must have "capital controls" in place so that you don't spend it all before your demise.

The way you preserve your wealth is buy par valued real estate with cash. This way the cash does not lose its value. You don't want to speculate in real estate with cash because the property may not go up in value. Real estate is a drain on your cash. It's cash intensive. The second thing you will want to do is create a type of monthly budget so that you don't go over that limit. The third thing you don't want to do is spend on expensive items that will drain your cash like buying a broken plane or a multi-million dollar yacht. These stupid purchases will make you broke because they are depreciating assets.

The way to preserve your money is to keep it in an interest bearing account. Invest in inexpensive start-ups with small amounts of capital. Retain a budget. Use your money to create assets instead of necessarily buying assets. Become a performer in entertainment where you get paid for your performance.

Rule of thumb, develop as much skill imaginable without the use of money first, than get involved in a low overhead business that generates a profit. Afterward, when your business acumen is sharpened you may use financial leverage and other instruments to capitalize your way into bigger business.

CHAPTER 14: *SOMEONE HAS IT*

"God will supply every need of yours."[xxviii]

Know this. Someone has what you need. Visualization is important to understand this concept. If you need free Internet just go to the library. If you want free tickets then you need to have a contact that has those free tickets. If want to go hot tubbing at a resort, than know someone who has access and is willing to let you in. If you need a place to stay, make sure to network with friends who can turn that into a reality.

The key is to be a person of source. Make sure you have a lot to offer too. This way you can exchange assistance. The bartering of time for services rendered is very helpful when people need you. You are a body and that is good enough. Many times your presence is required to help move something or keep someone company. Your voice is not really needed; it's just your presence. Your home, car, or contacts are things people will want to tap into so know how to leverage them to your advantage in bartering.

Have a large extensive network that is beneficial to you. You'll want to have friends in different cities and countries. This way they can always do something for you and vice a versa. Face it; if you don't have a large family it's best you widen your network of "obligatory assistance" by expanding your friend database. How many family members are worthless? Many. As of date, there are approximately 7.4 billion people on the planet, so you should not have a problem making friends. Make it a habit to generate tons of friends through unforced organic friendships.[xxix]

The way to expand your social database is to be sociable and open. There are so many people who limit their social interaction because they can't get off their high horse. There is no need to rule the room. Just seek out those who want to converse and feel out a connection. If there is a connection than convert it to a contact in your database. It's as simple as that. The one who is rich with contacts has many friends who will give him free assistance. Naturally, you will have to pay with gratitude in some kind of financial gift, but make it fun and not obligatory.

CHAPTER 15: *HIDE YOUR MONEY*

"In all labor there is profit, but mere talk leads only to poverty."[xxx]

Don't flaunt your money. This is a big no-no. It will only spur your competition more. First you must tuck away money. You need to keep your saved surplus as far as possible from the point of sale. For example, shopping malls are classic examples of points of sale. Essentially, you are walking into a landmine of things to buy. It comes with the territory. The same goes with a supermarket – lots of things to buy. In these two cases you better exercise some discipline or your money will be gone. Worse, if you are in possession of a credit card you will always be susceptible to spending at ease. So remember that point of sale is where you lose money. It's not your friend but your enemy.

The best thing you can do is stay in cash. It allows you to spend infrequently so that you don't splurge. Also, begin to buy crypto-currency. The reason why these investments are worth it is because there is a high demand. If it were not so, then you could not make money from the investment because there is not another fool ready to purchase the good at the new price. Your crypto-currency account is not public to the world. Realize this, great wealth is attained quietly. It's not for everyone to see.

Flex your muscles with the purchase of real estate in cash, business formation, and travel. People who can't afford these luxuries will begin to feel your money power and respect you. Once they see you are way ahead of them, your success will provoke them to secretly become jealous of you and they will want to be like you. The game is to cheap it; not keep it. There you have it. You have been enriched. Now, get rich and make me proud!

CONCLUSION:

"So every good tree bears good fruit, but the bad tree bears bad fruit."[xxxi]

Enclosed is an elegant photo of my luxury midrise condominium community in Las Vegas, Nevada.[xxxii] I paid cash for my unit. I bought my property for a song and a dance too. It's grown in equity over the years. The money is safe because it is stored away in a reliable asset.

I go to the pool often during the summertime; I use the gym when I want to, and I love to go hot tubbing, watching the stars in the evening during the wintertime. Occasionally, a shooting star zooms in the night. Often, I chuckle to myself and a big grin envelops my face, then a twinkle in my eye sheds a tear and I ask that unpretentious question, “How am I so privileged? Here is the answer. I have wholeheartedly listened to the wisdom of others who were before me. They have imparted prodigious sagacity to me over the years.

You must enjoy the fruit of your labor. I show you this fruit as evidence because I have employed keen fundamentals to afford a high standard of life. The accomplishment is the practice of frugality and living intelligently. We live in a society that should reward those who earned it by merit. I have done it correctly. I have cheated no one. I have played the game right. I have evidence that shows success. If it were not so, this book would be a sham. Follow suit my friend. I am before you.

BLESSING:

If you say, "The Lord is my refuge,"
and you make the Most High your dwelling,
10 no harm will overtake you,
no disaster will come near your tent.
11 For he will command his angels concerning you
to guard you in all your ways;
12 they will lift you up in their hands,
so that you will not strike your foot against a stone.
13 You will tread on the lion and the cobra;
you will trample the great lion and the serpent.
14 "Because he loves me," says the Lord, "I will rescue him;
I will protect him, for he acknowledges my name.
15 He will call on me, and I will answer him;

I will be with him in trouble,
I will deliver him and honor him.
16 With long life I will satisfy him
and show him my salvation."[xxxiii]

NOTES

[i] Proverbs 11:25

[ii] http://www.dictionary.com/browse/cheap

[iii] Proverbs 13:12

[iv] Proverbs 23:23

[v] Exodus 1:10

[vi] Luke 15:14

[vii] Lostitutes" is the plural form of "lostitute," a neologism coined by Sean Christopher.

[viii] Lostitution" is a neologism coined by Sean Christopher

[ix] http://www.bbc.com/travel/story/20120816-travelwise-casino-design-and-why-the-house-always-wins

[x] http://articles.orlandosentinel.com/1994-08-18/news/9408170495_1_chris-gutierrez-pagan-chuck-williams

[xi] Matthew 21:22

[xii] Goodwill Industries

[xiii] Some say, "Just buy it because it saves time." However, life is a journey. It's great to see things pop up out of nowhere when you employ *delayed gratification*. This is not always possible based on

extenuating circumstances.
[xiv] Mark 4:28
[xv] https://www.dennisbono.com
[xvi] Proverbs 30:25
[xvii] Had you invested in Bitcoin early you would be a Bitcoin millionaire today.
[xviii] Ecclesiastes 11:1
[xix] https://www.thegoldandoilguy.com/stock-market-elliott-wave-count-economic-cycle-equities-cycle/
[xx] Galatians 6:10
[xxi] Matthew 25:23
[xxii] Proverbs 10:14
[xxiii] "Caught up" means *to be enthralled or mired in something.*
[xxiv] II Chronicles 9:22
[xxv] https://www.fumoney.com/ebook
[xxvi]The conversation around FU Money is concentrated on how much does it denote? Certain books and articles posit the amount is over 10 million dollars.
[xxvii] Proverbs 13:22
[xxviii] Philippians 4:19
[xxix] http://www.worldometers.info/world-population/
[xxx] Proverbs 14:23
[xxxi] Matthew 7:17
[xxxii] GLVAR 2016
[xxxiii] Psalm 91:9-16

Made in the USA
Coppell, TX
04 November 2026

11278085R00031